NATIONAL GALLERY OF ART, WASHINGTON

An Illustrated Treasury of Songs

An Illustrated

NATIONAL GALLERY OF ART, WASHINGTON

Treasury of Songs

 **Hal Leonard Publishing Corporation**

7777 West Bluemound Road P.O. Box 13819 Milwaukee, WI 53213

RIZZOLI NEW YORK

First published in the United States of America in 1991
by Rizzoli International Publications, Inc.
300 Park Avenue South, New York, New York 10010
Copyright © 1991 Rizzoli International Publications, Inc.
Music and lyrics copyright © 1991 Hal Leonard Publishing Corporation
Illustrations copyright © 1991 National Gallery of Art, Washington D.C.

Designed by Nai Y. Chang
Printed and bound in Singapore

Library of Congress Cataloging-in-Publication Data

An illustrated treasury of songs: National Gallery of Art
55 scores
Traditional songs for voice and piano.
Includes chord symbols.
ISBN 0-8478-1376-2
1. Folk music—United States.   2. Folk-songs, English—United
States.   3. Songs with piano.
M1629.046   1991   90-755274
                                                          CIP
                                                           M

FRONT COVER AND
TITLE PAGE ILLUSTRATION

Henri Matisse, 1869-1954
Pianist and Checker Players (1924)
Canvas, 0.737 × 0.924 m (29 × 36⅜ in.)
National Gallery of Art, Washington
Collection of Mr. and Mrs. Paul Mellon
1985.64.25

BACK COVER ILLUSTRATION

Edward Hicks, 1780-1849
The Cornell Farm (1848)
Canvas, 0.933 × 1.244 m (36¾ × 49 in.)
National Gallery of Art, Washington
Gift of Edgar Willam and Bernice Chrysler Garbisch
1964.23.4

FRONTISPIECE

Tailpiece from *Estampes pour servir a l'Histoire des Moeurs
et du Costume* (published 1783), National Gallery of Art, Washington
Widener Collection 1942.9.1789

CONTENTS

THOMAS HART BENTON
TRAIL RIDERS, 1964/1965

ON TOP OF OLD SMOKY

Appalachian

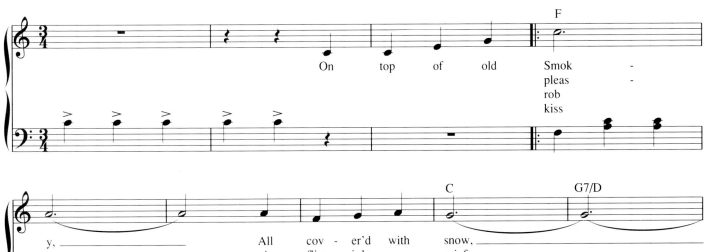

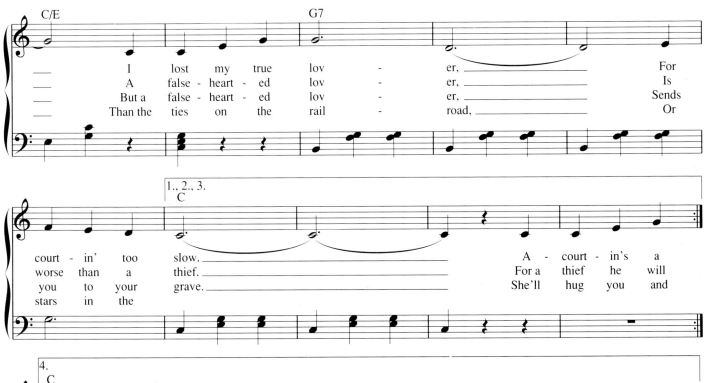

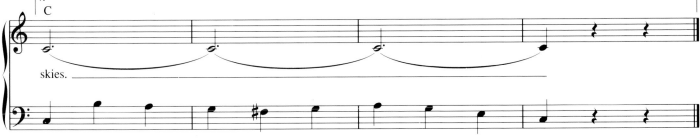

DOWN IN THE VALLEY

Appalachian Folk Song

1. Down in the val ley, Valley so low, Hang your head o - ver, Hear the wind blow,

2. Hear the wind blow, love, hear the wind

3. If you don't love me, love whom you please.
   Throw your arms 'round me, give my heart ease.

4. Give my heart ease, love, give my heart ease,
   Throw your arms 'round me, give my heart ease.

5. Write me a letter, send it by mail,
   Send it in care of the Birmingham Jail.

6. Birmingham Jail, love, Birmingham Jail.
   Send it in care of the Birmingham Jail.

THOMAS CHAMBERS
THE CONNECTICUT VALLEY, MID-19TH CENTURY

7. Build me a castle forty feet high,
   So I can see her as she rides by.

8. As she rides by, love, as she rides by,
   So I can see her as she rides by.

9. Roses love sunshine, violets love dew,
   Angels in heaven know I love you.

10. Know I love you, dear, know I love you,
   Angels in heaven know I love you.

THIS TRAIN

Gospel

With spirit

1. This train is bound for glo - ry, this train.

This train is bound for glo - ry, this train.

This train is rid - ing sole - ly for the mem - bers of the right-eous and the ho - ly.

This train is bound for glo - ry, this train.

2. This train takes no deceivers,
This train.
This train takes no deceivers,
This train.
This train takes no deceivers,
Takes no hypocrites and non-believers,
This train is bound for glory, this train!

3. This train don't carry no fakers,
This train.
This train don't carry no fakers,
This train.
Won't stop for cheatin' fakers,
Idle gossips and trouble makers,
This train is bound for glory, this train!

4. This train don't carry meddlers,
This train.
This train don't carry meddlers,
This train.
Won't stop for mischievous meddlers,
Gives no tickets to narcotic peddlers,
This train is bound for glory, this train!

GEORGE INNESS
THE LACKAWANNA VALLEY, 1855

5. This train don't carry sinners,
   This train.
   This train don't carry sinners,
   This train.
   This train don't carry sinners,
   No prevaricating tall-tale spinners,
   This train is bound for glory, this train!

6. So if you want to ride on
    this train,
   Look who you'll sit beside on
    this train;
   Folks who their ways have mended,
   Folks who live the way the Lord intended,
   This train is bound for glory, this train!

7. And if you qualify for
    this train,
   You'll need no pass to buy for
    this train.
   Be kind, be fair and patient,
   Show your neighbor no discrimination,
   This train is bound for glory, this train!

ANONYMOUS AMERICAN
BOSTON AND NORTH CHUNGAHOCHIE EXPRESS, AFTER 1916/1919

I'VE BEEN WORKING ON THE RAILROAD

Carmina Princetonia (1894)

Vigorously

I've been work-ing on the rail - road, All the live long day;

I've been work-ing on the rail - road, just to pass the time a - way.

Can't you hear the whis- tle blow - in'? Rise up so ear - ly in the morn.

Can't you hear the cap - tain shout - in' "Di - nah, blow your horn!"

Di - nah won't you blow Di - nah won't you blow Di - nah won't you blow your horn?____

HICKORY DICKORY DOCK

English Folk Song

Lively

Hick - o - ry, dick - o - ry, dock! The mouse ran up the clock. The

clock struck one and down he run. Hick - o - ry, dick - o - ry, dock!

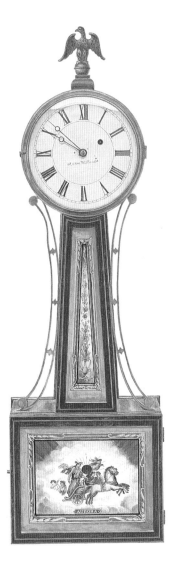

RENDERED BY FRANK KEANE
BANJO CLOCK, 1805-1815

THE VILLAGE BLACKSMITH

Traditional

Moderately

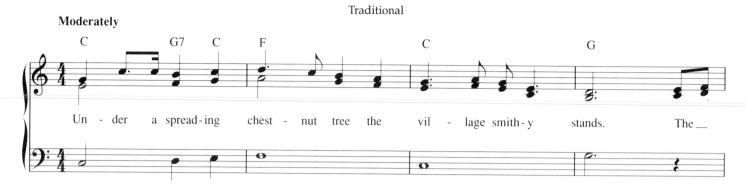

Un - der a spread-ing chest - nut tree the vil - lage smith-y stands. The __

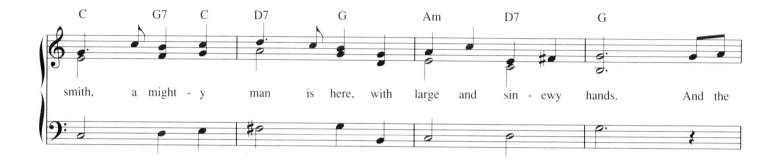

smith, a might - y man is here, with large and sin - ewy hands. And the

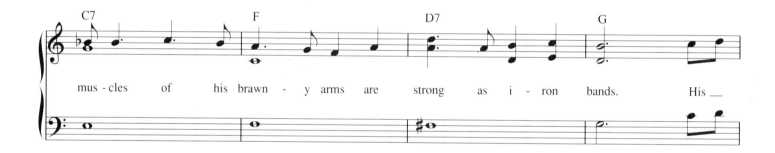

mus - cles of his brawn - y arms are strong as i - ron bands. His __

hair is crisp and black and long, his __ face is like the tan. His

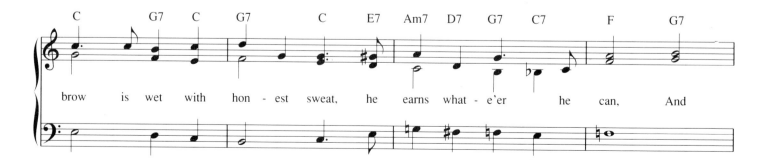

brow is wet with hon - est sweat, he earns what - e'er he can, And

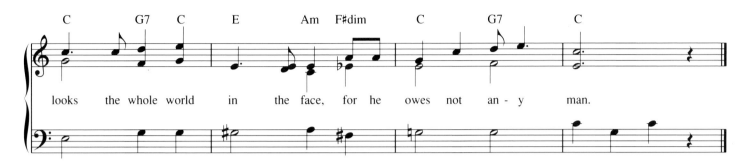

looks the whole world in the face, for he owes not an - y man.

THÉODORE GÉRICAULT
THE FLEMISH FARRIER, 1821

CAMPTOWN RACES

Words and Music by STEPHEN FOSTER

The camp - town la - dies sing this song, Doo - dah!
long - tail fil - ly and the big black horse, Doo - dah!

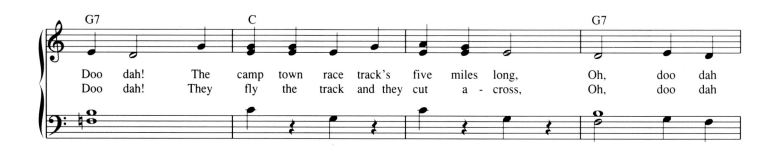

Doo dah! The camp town race track's five miles long, Oh, doo dah
Doo dah! They fly the track and they cut a - cross, Oh, doo dah

day! I came down there with my hat caved in,
day! The blind horse stuck in a big mud hole,

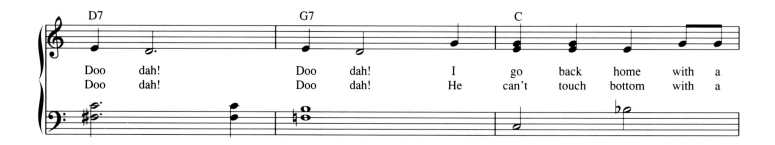

Doo dah! Doo dah! I go back home with a
Doo dah! Doo dah! He can't touch bottom with a

pock et full of tin, Oh, doo dah - day!
ten - foot pole, Oh, doo dah - day!   Goin' to run all

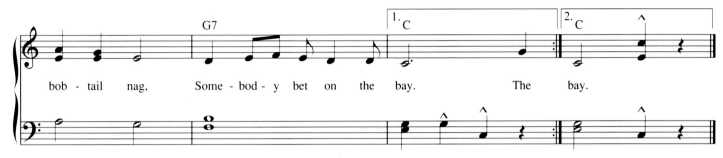

night, Goin' to run all day; I'll __ bet my mon-ey on the bob-tail nag, Some-bod-y bet on the bay. The bay.

ANONYMOUS AMERICAN
THE FINISH, C. 1860

THE FARMER

1. The farm – er in the dell, The farm – er in the dell,
2. The farm – er takes a wife, The farm – er takes a wife,

3. The wife takes a child, etc.
4. The child takes a nurse, etc.
5. The nurse takes a dog, etc.
6. The dog takes a cat, etc.
7. The cat takes a rat, etc.
8. The rat takes the cheese, etc.
9. The cheese stands alone, etc.

N THE DELL

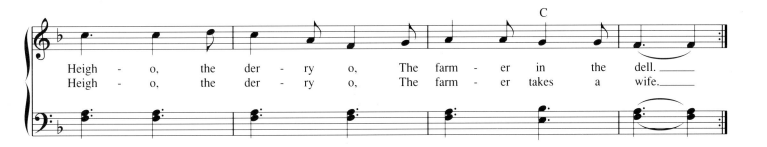

Heigh - o, the der - ry o, The farm - er in the dell._____
Heigh - o, the der - ry o, The farm - er takes a wife._____

ANONYMOUS AMERICAN
MAHANTANGO VALLEY FARM, LATE 19TH CENTURY

OLD MACDONALD

Traditional

Moderately

1. Old Mac - Don - ald had a farm, E I E I O! And
2. Old Mac - Don - ald had a farm, E I E I O! And

on his farm he had some chicks, E I E I O! With a
on his farm he had some cows, E I E I O! With a

3. Old MacDonald had a farm,
   E-I-E-I-O,
   And on his farm he had a horse,
   E-I-E-I-O.
   With a neigh-neigh here and a neigh-neigh there, *etc.*

4. Old MacDonald had a farm,
   E-I-E-I-O,
   And on his farm he had a donkey,
   E-I-E-I-O.
   With a hee-haw here, *etc.*

For additional verses, add your own animals.

HAD A FARM

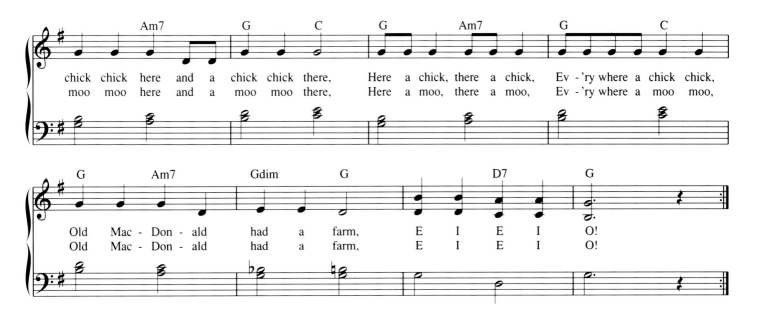

chick chick here and a chick chick there, Here a chick, there a chick, Ev-'ry where a chick chick,
moo moo here and a moo moo there, Here a moo, there a moo, Ev-'ry where a moo moo,

Old Mac-Don-ald had a farm, E I E I O!
Old Mac-Don-ald had a farm, E I E I O!

EDWARD HICKS
THE CORNELL FARM, 1848

HENRI DE TOULOUSE-LAUTREC
THE ARTIST'S DOG FLÈCHE, C. 1881

BINGO

English Folk Song

OH WHERE, OH WHERE HAS MY LITTLE DOG GONE?

Words by SEPTIMUS WINNER
German Folk Song

ANONYMOUS AMERICAN
THE DOG, EARLY 20TH CENTURY

THREE LITTLE KITTENS

Traditional

Three Lit - tle Kit - tens lost their mit - tens, And they be - gan to
Three Lit - tle Kit - tens found their mit - tens, And they be - gan to
Three Lit - tle Kit - tens put on their mit - tens, And soon ate up the
Three Lit - tle Kit - tens washed their mit - tens, And hung them up to

cry, _____ Oh! moth - er dear, We great - ly fear, Our
cry, _____ Oh! moth - er dear, See here, see here, Our
pie, _____ Oh! moth - er dear, We great - ly fear, Our
dry, _____ Oh! moth - er dear, Look here, look here, Our

mit - tens we have lost _____ What! Lost your mit - tens? You
mit - tens we have found _____ Put on your mit - tens, You
mit - tens we have soiled _____ What! Soiled your mit - tens? You
mit - tens we have washed _____ What! Washed your mit - tens? You

naugh - ty kit - tens, Then you shall have no pie.
sil - ly kit - tens, And you shall have some pie.
naugh - ty kit - tens, Then they be - gan to sigh.
dar - ling kit - tens, I smell a rat close by.

Mee - ow,

Mee - ow, Mee - ow, Mee - ow, Mee - ow,

ANONYMOUS AMERICAN
CAT AND KITTENS, C. 1872/1883

LITTLE MISS MUFFET

Mother Goose

Lit - tle Miss Muf - fet sat on a tuf - fet, eat - ing some curds and whey._____ There

came a big Spi - der and sat down be - side her, and fright - ened Miss Muf- fet a - way._____

WILLIAM MATTHEW PRIOR
LITTLE MISS FAIRFIELD, 1850

GUSTAV KLIMT
BABY (CRADLE), 1917/1918

ROCK-A-BYE BABY

Traditional

In a sleepy mood

Rock - a - bye ba - by, on the tree top. When the wind

blows, the cra - dle will rock. When the bough breaks, the

cra - dle will fall. And down will come ba - by cra - dle and all.

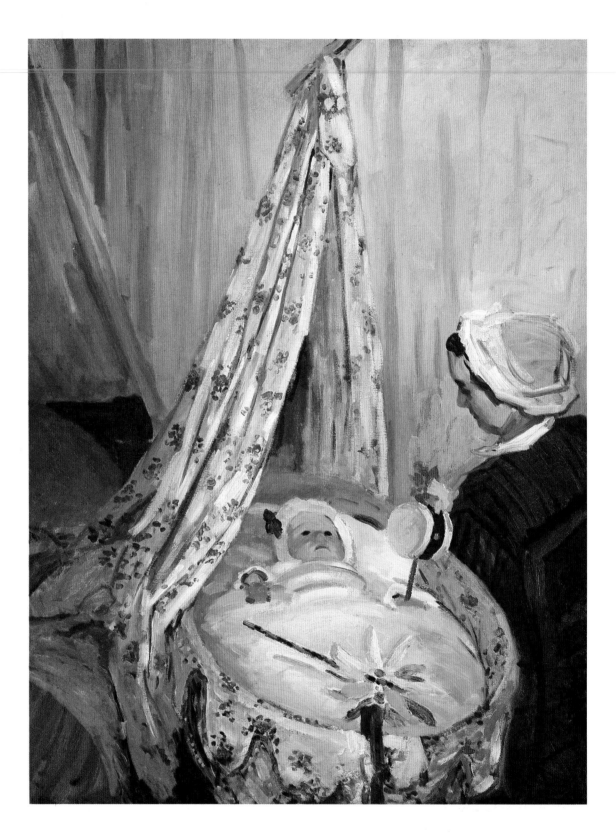

CLAUDE MONET
THE CRADLE—CAMILLE WITH THE ARTIST'S SON JEAN, 1867

HUSH, LITTLE BABY

Southern American Folk Song

2. If that diamond ring is brass,
   Papa's gonna buy you a looking glass,
   And if that looking glass should crack,
   Papa's gonna buy you a jumping jack.

3. If that jumping jack won't hop,
   Papa's gonna buy you a lollipop,
   When that lollipop is done,
   Papa's gonna buy you another one.

4. If that lollipop is all eaten up,
   Papa's gonna buy you a real live pup,
   If that puppy dog won't bark,
   Papa's gonna buy you a meadow lark.

5. If that diamond ring is glass,
   Papa's gonna buy you a cup of brass,
   And from that cup you'll drink your milk,
   And Papa's gonna dress you in the finest silk.

6. Yes, Papa's gonna dress you in the finest silk,
   And Mama's gonna raise you with honey and milk,
   So hush, little baby, sleep safe and sound,
   You're still the sweetest little babe in town.

TOYLAND

Word and Music by VICTOR HERBERT

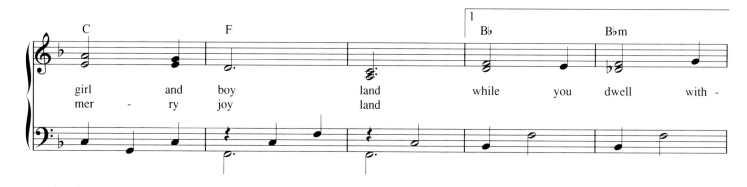

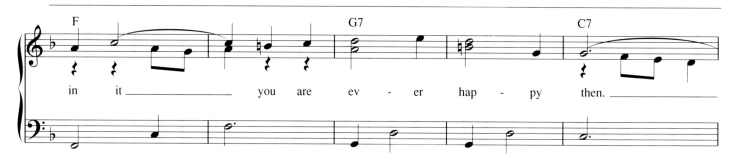

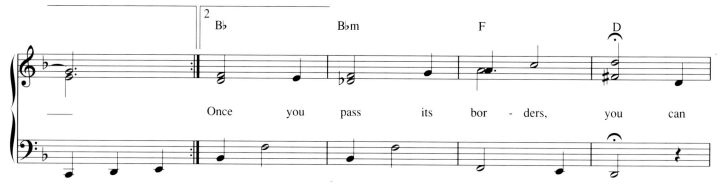

THOMAS EAKINS
BABY AT PLAY, 1876

SKIP TO MY LOU

Traditional

Bright square dance tempo

2. Lost my partner, what'll I do, (3 times)
   Chorus

3. I'll get another one prettier than you, (3 times)
   Chorus

4. Flies in the buttermilk, shoo, fly, shoo (3 times)
   Chorus

5. Little red wagon painted blue, (3 times)
   Chorus

6. Gone again, skip to my Lou. (3 times)
   Chorus

RENDERED BY KATHARINE MERRILL
DANCING GIRL FROM SPARK'S CIRCUS WAGON, C. 1900

RENDERED BY JANE IVERSON
WOODEN DOLL, C. 1800

BUFFALO GALS

Words and Music by COOL WHITE

2. I danced with a gal with a hole in her stocking
   And her heel kept a-knockin' and her toes kept a-
   rocking
   I danced with a gal with a hole in her stocking
   And we danced by the light of the moon.

GIT ALONG

Cowboy Song

Moderate Waltz Tempo

1. As I was a-walk-ing one morn-ing for pleas-ure, I spied a cow-punch-er a-stroll-in' a-long. His hat was throwed back and his spurs were a-jin-glin', and as he ap-proached he was sing-ing this song. Whoop-ee ti - yi-

2. Early in the springtime we'll round up the dogies,
Slap on their brands and bob off their tails;
Round up our horses, load up the chuck wagon,
Then throw those dogies upon the trail.

3. It's whooping and yelling and driving the dogies,
Oh, how I wish you would go on,
It's whooping and punching and go on, little dogies,
For you know Wyoming will be your new home.

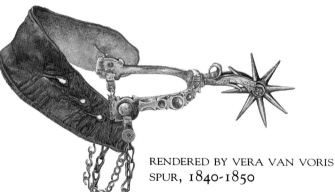

RENDERED BY VERA VAN VORIS
SPUR, 1840-1850

4. Some of the boys goes up the trail for pleasure,
But that's where they git it most awfully wrong;
For you haven't any idea the trouble they give us,
When we go driving them dogies along.

RENDERED BY ROSE CAMPBELL-GERKE
SPUR, C. 1890

LITTLE DOGIES

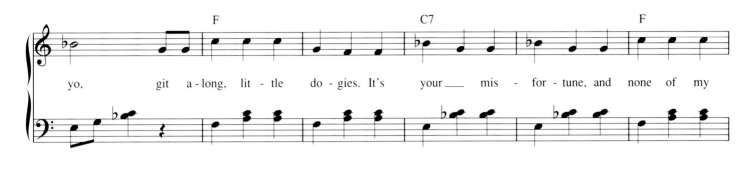

yo, git a - long, lit - tle do - gies. It's your ___ mis - for - tune, and none of my

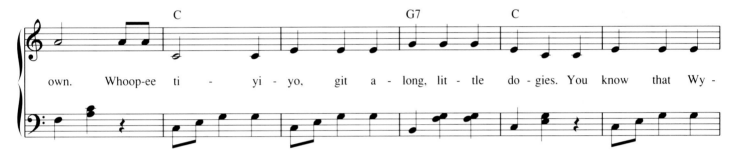

own. Whoop-ee ti - yi - yo, git a - long, lit - tle do - gies. You know that Wy -

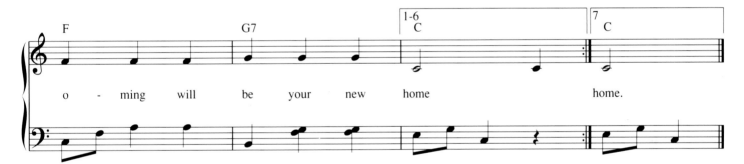

o - ming will be your new home home.

5. When the night comes on and we hold them
   on the bed-ground,
   These little dogies that roll on so slow;
   Roll up the herd and cut out the strays,
   And roll the little dogies that never rolled before.

RENDERED BY WILLIAM KIECKHOFEL
SPUR, C. 1880-1890

6. Your mother she was raised way down in Texas,
   Where the jimson weed and sandburs grow;
   Now we'll fill you up on prickly pear and cholla,
   Till you are ready for the trail to Idaho.

RENDERED BY RAYMOND E. NOBLE
SPUR, C. 1850

HOME ON THE RANGE

Words by JOHN HOWARD PAYNE
Music by SIR HENRY BISHOP

2. How often at night when the heavens are bright,
   From the light of the glittering stars,
   Have I stood there, amazed and asked as I gazed,
   If their glory exceeds that of ours.

3. Where the air is so pure and the zephyrs so free;
   And the breezes so balmy and light,
   Oh, I would not exchange my home on the range,
   For the glittering cities so bright.

4. Oh, give me a land where the bright diamond sand,
   Flows leisurely down with the stream,
   Where the graceful white swan glides slowly along,
   Like a maid in a heavenly dream.

HENRY MERWIN SHRADY
THE EMPTY SADDLE, 1900

GEORGE CATLIN
SNOW SHOE DANCE—OJIBBEWAY, 1861/1869

TEN LITTLE INDIANS

Words and Music by SEPTIMUS WINNER

LISTEN TO THE MOCKINGBIRD

Words and Music by ALICE HAWTHORNE

Moderately

I'm dream - ing now of sweet Hal - lie, __ my sweet Hal - lie, __ my sweet
sleep - ing down in the val - ley, __ in the val - ley, __ in the

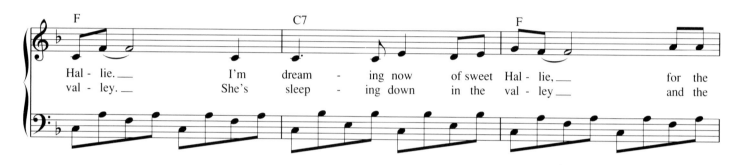

Hal - lie. __ I'm dream - ing now of sweet Hal - lie, __ for the
val - ley. __ She's sleep - ing down in the val - ley __ and the

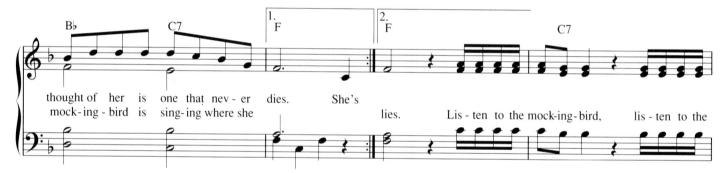

thought of her is one that nev - er dies. She's
mock - ing - bird is sing-ing where she lies. Lis - ten to the mock-ing-bird, lis - ten to the

mock - ing - bird, The mock - ing - bird is sing - ing o'er her grave. Lis - ten to the

mock-ing-bird, lis - ten to the mock-ing-bird, still sing - ing where the weep-ing wil - lows wave.

1. Mountain Mocking bird, Male.
ORPHEUS MONTANUS, Townsend

2. 3. Varied Thrush, Male & Female.
TURDUS NÆVIUS, Gm.

Plant Thicket
Designs Vaccinearum

Drawn from Nature by J. J. Audubon, F.R.S. F.L.S.

Engraved, Printed and Coloured by R. Havell 1837

JOHN JAMES AUDUBON
MOUNTAIN MOCKING-BIRD AND VARIED THRUSH, 1837

49

RING AROUND THE ROSY

Traditional

fly   to   the   one   that _____ you   love   best.

PAUL GAUGUIN
BRETON GIRLS DANCING, PONT-AVEN, 1888

A TISKET, A TASKET

Traditional

ANONYMOUS AMERICAN
BASKET OF FRUIT WITH FLOWERS, C. 1830

HENRI MATISSE
THE FUNERAL OF PIERROT, PUBLISHED 1947

WHEN THE SAINTS GO MARCHING IN

Spiritual

2. Oh, when the sun refuse to shine,
Oh, when the sun refuse to shine,
Oh Lord I want to be in that number,
When the sun refuse to shine.

3. Oh, when the stars have disappeared,
Oh, when the stars have disappeared,
Oh Lord I want to be in that number,
When the stars have disappeared.

4. Oh, when the day of judgement comes,
Oh, when the day of judgement comes,
Oh Lord I want to be in that number,
When the day of judgement comes.

SHE'LL BE COMIN'

Railroad Song

With spirit

1. She'll be com - in' 'round the moun - tain when she comes (when she comes) She'll be com - in' 'round the moun - tain when she comes (when she

2. She'll be drivin' six white horses
   when she comes, etc.

3. She'll be shinin' just like silver
   when she comes, etc.

4. Oh, we'll all go out to meet her
   when she comes, etc.

5. We'll be singin' hallelujah
   when she comes, etc.

6. We will kill the old red rooster
   when she comes, etc.

ROUND THE MOUNTAIN

(comes) She'll be com-in' 'round the moun-tain, She'll be com-in' 'round the moun-tain, She'll be com-in' 'round the moun-tain when she comes (when she comes).

RENDERED BY E. BOYD
PAINTED CHEST, C. 1810-1820

DID YOU EVER SEE A LASSIE?

Traditional

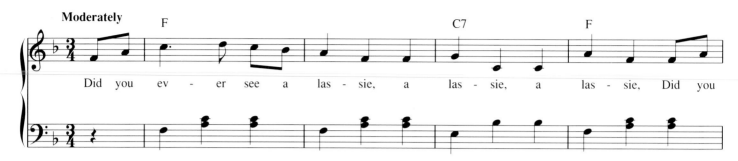

Did you ev - er see a las - sie, a las - sie, a las - sie, Did you

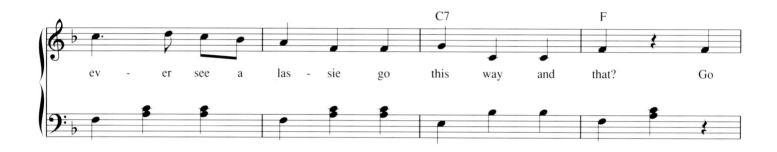

ev - er see a las - sie go this way and that? Go

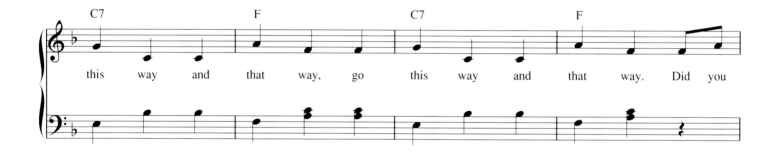

this way and that way, go this way and that way. Did you

ev - er see a las - sie go this way and that?

RENDERED BY E. BOYD
PAINTED CHEST, C. 1820

OH SUSANNA

Words and Music by STEPHEN FOSTER

THOMAS EAKINS
STUDY FOR "NEGRO BOY DANCING": THE BANJO PLAYER, C. 1878

2. I had a dream the other night,
   When everything was still
   I dreamed I saw Susanna
   A-coming down the hill.

3. A red red rose was in her cheek,
   A tear was in her eye
   I said to her, Susanna girl,
   Susanna don't you cry.

CLEMENTINE

Traditional

2. Light she was, and like a fairy, and her shoes were number nine,
   Herring boxes without topses, sandals were for Clementine.
   Chorus

3. Drove she ducklings to the water every morning just at nine,
   Hit her foot against a splinter, fell into the foaming brine.
   Chorus

4. Ruby lips above the water, blowing bubbles soft and fine,
   Alas for me! I was no swimmer, so I lost my Clementine.
   Chorus

RENDERED BY JOSEPHINE ROMANO AND EDITH TOWNER
DOLL, "MOLLIE BENTLEY", C. 1886

HENRI MATISSE
STILL LIFE WITH SLEEPING WOMAN, 1940

BEAUTIFUL DREAMER

Words and Music by STEPHEN FOSTER

Beautiful dreamer, out on the sea
Mermaids are chanting the wild Lorelei,
Over the streamlet vapors are borne
Waiting to fade at the bright coming morn.
Beautiful dreamer, beam on my heart
E'en as the morn on the streamlet and sea,
Then will all clouds of sorrow depart.
Beautiful dreamer, awake unto me.

MAN ON THE FLYING TRAPEZE

Words by GEORGE LEYBOURNE
Music by ALFRED LEE

JOHN MARIN
UNTITLED: CIRCUS, C. 1953

Moderate Waltz

1. Oh, once I was hap-py, but now I'm for-lorn, like an old coat that is tat-tered and torn. Left in this wide world to fret and to mourn, be-trayed by a maid in her teens. — Oh, the girl that I loved, she was hand-some and I tried all I knew her to please, but I could not

2. Now the young man by name was Señor Boni Slang,
Tall, big and handsome, as well made as Chang.
Where'er he appeared, how the hall loudly rang,
With ovations from all people there.
He'd smile from the bar on the people below
And one night he smiled on my love,
She winked back at him, and she shouted, "Bravo!"
As he hung by his nose from above.

3. Her father and mother were both on my side
And tried very hard to make her my bride.
Her father, he sighed, and her mother, she cried
To see her throw herself away.
'Twas all no avail, she went there ev'ry night
And threw her bouquets on the stage,
Which caused him to meet her – how he ran me down,
To tell it would take a whole page.

4. One night I as usual went to her dear home,
   And found there her mother and father alone.
   I asked for my love, and soon 'twas made known,
   To my horror, that she'd run away.
   She packed up her boxes and eloped in the night,
   With him with the greatest of ease.
   From two stories high he had lowered her down
   To the ground on his flying trapeze.

5. Some months after that I went into a hall;
   To my surprise I found there on the wall
   A bill in red letters which did my heart gall,
   That she was appearing with him.
   He'd taught her gymnastics, and dressed her in tights
   To help him live at ease.
   He'd made her assume a masculine name,
   And now she goes on the trapeze.

Final chorus:
      She floats through the air with the greatest of ease;
      You'd think her a man on the flying trapeze.
      She does all the work while he takes his ease,
      And that's what's become of my love.

WHILE STROLLING THROUGH

Words and Music by ED HALEY

Moderately

THE PARK ONE DAY

lov - ly af - ter - noon I _____ met her at the foun - tain in the park.

MAURICE BRAZIL PRENDERGAST
SALEM COVE, 1916

GREENSLEEVES

Elizabethan

1. A las, my love ____ you do me wrong, ____ To cast me off ____ dis-
I have loved ____ you oh, so long, ____ De-

2.-4. *(See additional lyrics)*

cour - teous - ly, And light - ing in ____ your com - pa - ny.

Green - sleeves ____ was all my joy, _____ Green - sleeves ____ was
Green - sleeves was my heart of gold, ____ And

my de - light. who but my la - dy Green - sleeves.

2. I have been ready at your hand,
   To grant whatever you would crave;
   I have both wagered life and land,
   Your love and good-will for to have.
   If you intend thus to disdain,
   It does the more enrapture me,
   And even so, I still remain
   A lover in captivity.

3. My men were clothed all in green,
   And they did ever wait on thee;
   All this was gallant to be seen;
   And yet thou wouldst not love me.
   Thou couldst desire no earthly thing
   But still thou hadst it readily.
   Thy music still to play and sing;
   And yet thou wouldst not love me.

4. Well, I will pray to God on high,
   That my constancy mayst see,
   And that yet once before I die,
   Thou wilt vouchsafe to love me.
   Ah, Greensleeves, now farewell, adieu,
   To God I pray to prosper thee,
   For I am still thy lover true,
   Come once again and love me.

GERARD TERBORCH II
THE SUITOR'S VISIT, C. 1658

OH DEAR! WHAT CAN THE MATTER BE?

Scottish Folk Song

Brightly

1. Oh, dear! What can the mat-ter be? Oh, dear! What can the mat-ter be?

Oh, dear! What can the mat-ter be? John-ny's so long at the fair. _____ 1. He

prom-ised to bring me a bas-ket of po-sies, a gar-land of lil-lies, a gar-land of ros-es. He

prom-ised to bring me a bunch of blue rib-bons to tie up my bon-nie brown hair.

2. He promised he'd buy me a gift that would please me
And then for a kiss, oh, he vowed he would tease me;
He promised he'd buy me a bunch of blue ribbons,
To tie up my bonnie brown hair.

WINSLOW HOMER
UNDER A PALM TREE, 1886

THE RIDDLE SONG

Traditional

2. How can there be a cherry that has no stone?
   How can there be a chicken that has no bone?
   How can there be a story that has no end?
   How can there be a baby with no cryin'?

3. A cherry, when it's blooming, it has no stone.
   A chicken, when it's piping, it has no bone.
   The story that I love you, it has no end.
   A baby, when it's sleeping, has no cryin'.

AUGUSTE RENOIR
PICKING FLOWERS, 1875

TELL ME WHY

Traditional

CLAUDE MONET
WOMAN WITH A PARASOL—MADAME MONET AND HER SON, 1875

LET ME CALL YOU SWEETHEART

Words by BETH SLATER WILSON
Music by LEO FREIDMAN

CLAUDE MONET
BAZILLE AND CAMILLE, 1865

ANDRE DERAIN
CHARING CROSS BRIDGE, LONDON, 1906

LONDON BRIDGE

English Folk Song

3. Build it up with sticks and stones,
   Sticks and stones, sticks and stones,
   Build it up with sticks and stones,
   My fair lady.

4. Sticks and stones will bend and break,
   Bend and break, Bend and break,
   Sticks and stones will bend and break,
   My fair lady.

5. Build it up with iron bars,
   Iron bars, iron bars,
   Build it up with iron bars,
   My fair lady.

6. Iron bars will rust away,
   Rust away, Rust away,
   Iron bars will rust away,
   My fair lady.

THE MULBERRY BUSH

English Folk Song

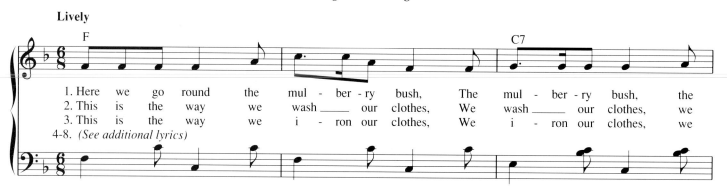

1. Here we go round the mul - ber - ry bush, The mul - ber - ry bush, the
2. This is the way we wash ____ our clothes, We wash ____ our clothes, we
3. This is the way we i - ron our clothes, We i - ron our clothes, we

4-8. *(See additional lyrics)*

mul - ber - ry bush. Here we go round the mul - ber - ry bush So
wash ____ our clothes. This is the way we wash ____ our clothes So
i - ron our clothes. This is the way we i - ron our clothes So

ear - ly in ____ the morn - ing. morn - ing.
ear - ly Mon - day morn - ing.
ear - ly Tues - day morn - ing.

4. This is the way we scrub the floor, *etc.*
   So early Wednesday morning.

5. This is the way we mend our clothes, *etc.*
   So early Thursday morning.

6. This is the way we sweep the house, *etc.*
   So early Friday morning.

7. This is the way we bake our bread, *etc.*
   So early Saturday morning.

8. This is the way we go to church, *etc.*
   So early Sunday morning.

EDGAR DEGAS
WOMAN IRONING, 1882

HOME SWEET HOME

Words by DR. BREWSTER HIGLEY
Music by DANIEL E. KELLY

RENDERED BY PERKINS HARNLY
"CALIFORNIA MISSION STYLE" INTERIOR, 1910-1911

2. An exile from home, splendor dazzles in vain,
   Oh, give me my lowly thatched cottage again;
   The birds singing gaily, that come at my call;
   Give me them, with that peace of mind, dearer than all.

3. To thee, I'll return, overburdened with care,
   The heart's dearest solace will smile on me there.
   No more from that cottage again will I roam,
   Be it ever so humble, there's no place like home.

GUSTAVE CAILLEBOTTE
SKIFFS, 1877

ROW, ROW, ROW YOUR BOAT

Traditional

CRAWDAD SONG

Traditional

Brightly

1. You get a line and I'll get a pole,___ Hon - ey, _____
2-6. *(See additional lyrics)*

You get a line and I'll get a pole,___ babe, _____

You get a line and I'll get a pole, We'll go down to the craw - dad hole,

Hon - ey, Oh, ba - by of mine. _____

2. Yonder comes a man with a pack on his back, honey,
   Yonder comes a man with a pack on his back, babe,
   Yonder comes a man with a pack on his back,
   Totin' all the crawdads he can pack,
   Honey, Oh baby of mine.

(continue similarly)

3. Sittin' on the ice till my feet got hot (3 times)
   Watchin' those crawdads rack and trot

4. Crawdad, crawdad, better go to your hole (3 times)
   If I don't catch you, well bless my soul!

5. Whatcha gonna do when the lake runs dry? (3 times)
   Sit on the bank and watch the crawdads die.

6. Whatcha gonna do when your man (gal) runs away?
   (3 times)
   Get you a better one the very next day.

WINSLOW HOMER
CASTING, NUMBER TWO, 1894

SAILING, SAILING

Words and Music by GODFREY MARKS

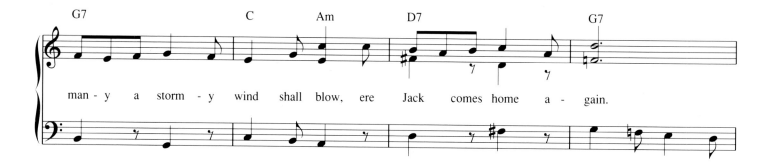

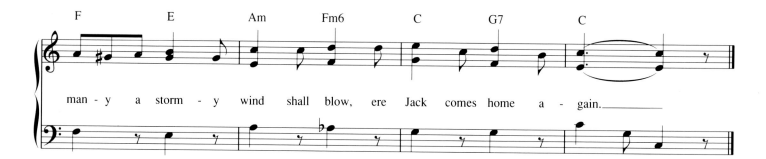

WINSLOW HOMER
BREEZING UP (A FAIR WIND), 1876

L. M. COOKE
SALUTE TO GENERAL WASHINGTON IN NEW YORK HARBOR,
FOURTH QUARTER 19TH CENTURY

BLOW THE MAN DOWN

Sea Chantey

2. As I was a-walkin' down Paradise Street,
   To me way! hey! — Blow the man down!
   A pretty young damsel I chanced for to meet,
   Give me some time to blow the man down.

3. She hailed me with her flipper, I took her in tow,
   To me way! hey! — Blow the man down!
   Yard-arm to yard-arm away we did go,
   Give me some time to blow the man down.

4. As soon as that Packet was clear of the bar,
   To me way! hey! — Blow the man down!
   The mate knocked me down with the end of a spar,
   Give me some time to blow the man down.

5. It's yard-arm to yard-arm away you will sprawl,
   Way! hey! — Blow the man down!
   For kicking Jack Rogers commands the Black Ball,
   Give me some time to blow the man down.

WHEN JOHNNY COMES

Words and Music by PATRICK S. GILMORE

Slow march

When John - ny comes march - ing home a - gain, Hur - rah!____ Hur - rah!____ We'll
The old church bell will peal with joy, Hur - rah!____ Hur - rah!____ To

give him a heart - y wel - come then, Hur - rah!____ Hur - rah!____ The __
wel - come home our dar - ling boy, Hur - rah!____ Hur - rah!____ The __

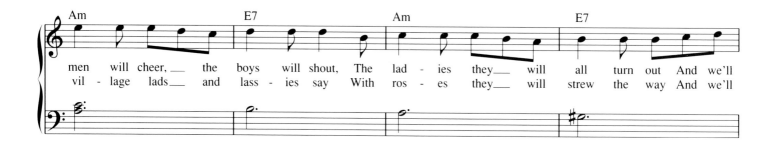

men will cheer, __ the boys will shout, The lad - ies they__ will all turn out And we'll
vil - lage lads__ and lass - ies say With ros - es they__ will strew the way And we'll

all feel gay when John - ny comes march - ing home.____
all feel gay when John - ny comes march - ing home.____

MARCHING HOME

RENDERED BY WAYNE WHITE
CIVIL WAR DRUM, C. 1860

YOU'RE A GRAND OLD FLAG

Words and Music by GEORGE M. COHAN

You're a grand old flag, tho' you're torn to a rag, And for-ev-er in peace may you wave. You're the em-blem of the land I love, The home of the free and the brave. Ev-'ry heart beats true un-der Red, White and

Blue, Where there's nev - er a boast or brag; ____ But "Should auld ac - quain - tance be for - got." Keep your eye on the grand old flag. ____

RENDERED BY ALFRED H. SMITH
EAGLE, 19TH CENTURY

JASPER FRANCIS CROPSEY
AUTUMN—ON THE HUDSON RIVER, 1860

AMERICA, THE BEAUTIFUL

Words by KATHERINE LEE BATES
Music by SAMUEL A. WARD

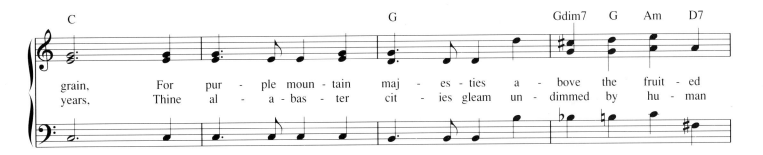

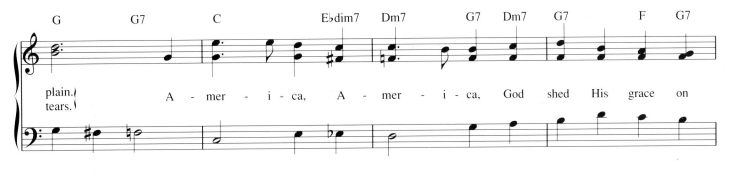

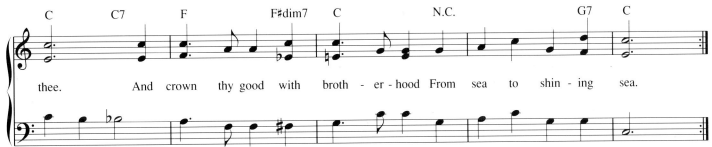

2. Oh beautiful for pilgrim feet
   Whose stern impassioned stress
   A thoroughfare for freedom beat
   Across the wilderness.
   America! America!
   God mend thine every flaw,
   Confirm thy soul in self-control,
   Thy liberty in law.

3. Oh beautiful for heroes proved
   In liberating strife,
   Who more than self their country loved
   And mercy more than life.
   America! America!
   May God thy gold refine
   'Til all success be nobleness,
   And every gain divine.

4. Oh beautiful for patriot dream
   That sees beyond the years,
   Thine alabaster cities gleam,
   Undimmed by human tears.
   America! America!
   God shed his grace on thee
   And crown thy good with brotherhood
   From sea to shining sea.

THE STAR-SPANGLED BANNER

Words by FRANCIS SCOTT KEY   Music by JOHN STAFFORD SMITH

With dignity

Oh __ say can you see, By the dawn's ear - ly light. What so

proud - ly we hailed at the twi - light's last gleam - ing, Whose broad stripes and bright

stars Thro' the per - il - ous fight O'er the ram - parts we watched Were so

gal - lant - ly stream - ing, And the rock - ets red glare, The bombs burst - ing in

air Gave proof thru the night that our flag was still there. Oh

say does that __ star - span - gled ban - ner __ Yet __ wave __ O'er the

land _____ of the free and the home of the brave.

CHILDE HASSAM
ALLIES DAY, MAY 1917, 1917

DOWN BY THE OLD MILL STREAM

Words and Music by TELL TAYLOR

Down by the old mill stream _____ where I first met you _____ with your eyes of blue _____ dressed in ging - ham too. _____ It was there I knew _____ that you loved me true. _____ You were six - teen, _____ my vil - lage queen, _____ down by the old

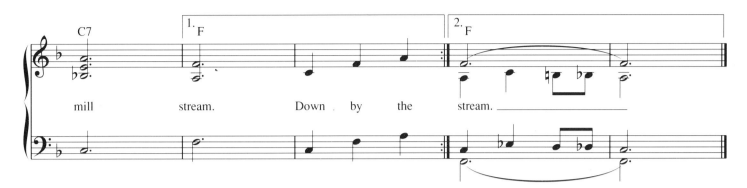

JEAN-BAPTISTE-CAMILLE COROT
FOREST OF FONTAINEBLEAU, C. 1830

JEAN-HONORÉ FRAGONARD
THE SWING, PROBABLY C. 1765

THE SWING

Spiritual

In a lilting rhythm

How do you like to go up in a swing, up in the
Up in the air _____ and o - ver the wall till I can
Till I look down on the gar - den green, down on the

air so blue? _____ Oh, I do think it the
see so wide, _____ Riv - ers and trees _____ and
roof so brown. _____ Up in the air I go

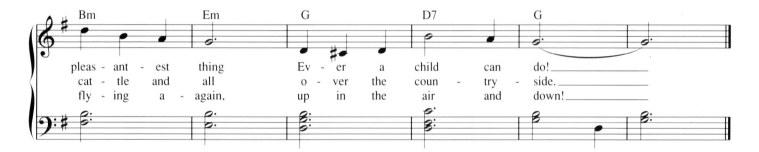

pleas - ant - est thing Ev - er a child can do! _____
cat - tle and all o - ver the coun - try - side. _____
fly - ing a - gain, up in the air and down! _____

SCHOOL DAYS

Words by WILL D. COBB
Music by GUS EDWARDS

love you, Joe." When we were a cou - ple of kids._____

PIERRE BONNARD
CHILDREN LEAVING SCHOOL, C. 1895

HALLOWEEN SONG

AFTER WILLIAM JOHN WILGUS
ICHABOD CRANE AND THE HEADLESS HORSEMAN, C. 1855

THIS OLD MAN

English Folk Song

4. This old man, he played four;
   He played knick-knack on my door.
   Chorus

5. This old man, he played five;
   He played knick-knack on my hive.
   Chorus

6. This old man, he played six;
   He played knick-knack on my sticks.
   Chorus

7. This old man, he played seven;
   He played knick-knack up in heaven.
   Chorus

8. This old man, he played eight;
   He played knick-knack on my gate.
   Chorus

9. This old man, he played nine;
   He played knick-knack on my spine.
   Chorus

10. This old man, he played ten;
    He played knick-knack once again.
    Chorus

JOHN QUIDOR
THE RETURN OF RIP VAN WINKLE, C. 1849

FRANCES FLORA BOND PALMER
AMERICAN WINTER SCENES: MORNING, PUBLISHED 1854

OVER THE RIVER AND THROUGH THE WOODS

Traditional

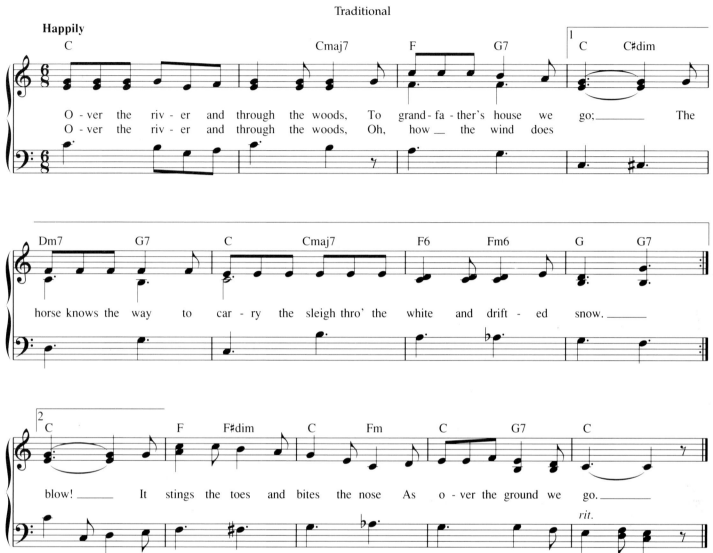

JINGLE BELLS

Words and Music by JAMES S. PIERPONT

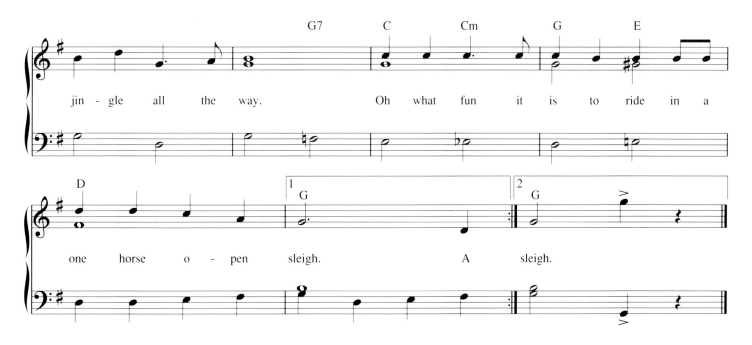

jin - gle all the way.   Oh what fun it is to ride in a

one horse o - pen sleigh.   A sleigh.

AFTER WINSLOW HOMER
CHRISTMAS BELLES, PUBLISHED 1869

FRANK STELLA
STAR OF PERSIA I, 1967

TWINKLE, TWINKLE, LITTLE STAR

Words by JANE TAYLOR
Traditional

LIST OF ILLUSTRATIONS

Anonymous American 19th Century
Basket of Fruit with Flowers (c. 1830)
wood, 0.351 × 0.455 m (13¾ × 17⅞ in.)
National Gallery of Art, Washington
Gift of Edgar William and Bernice Chrysler Garbisch
1980.62.43

Anonymous American 19th Century
Cat and Kittens (c. 1872/1883)
millboard, 0.300 × 0.350 m (11¾ × 13¾ in.)
National Gallery of Art, Washington
Gift of Edgar William and Bernice Chrysler Garbisch
1958.9.8

Anonymous American 19th Century
The Finish (c. 1860)
oil on wood, 0.587 × 0.952 m (23⅛ × 37½ in.)
National Gallery of Art, Washington
Gift of Edgar William and Bernice Chrysler Garbisch
1980.61.9

Anonymous American 19th Century
Mahantango Valley Farm (late 19th century)
canvas, 0.711 × 0.917 m (28 × 36⅛ in.)
Gift of Edgar William and Bernice Chrysler Garbisch
1953.5.93

Anonymous American 20th Century
Boston and North Chungahochie Express (after 1916/1919)
oil or tempera on composition board, 0.470 × 0.623 m
(18½ × 24½ in.)
National Gallery of Art, Washington
Gift of Edgar William and Bernice Chrysler Garbisch
1971.83.12

Anonymous American 20th Century
The Dog (early 20th century)
canvas, 0.895 × 1.054 m (35¼ × 41½ in.)
National Gallery of Art, Washington
Gift of Edgar William and Bernice Chrysler Garbisch
1957.11.8

John James Audubon, 1785-1851
Mountain Mocking-bird and Varied Thrush (1837)
hand-colored engraving with aquatint,
0.502 × 0.369 m (19¾ × 14½ in.)
National Gallery of Art, Washington
Gift of Mrs. Walter B. James 1945.8.369

Thomas Hart Benton, 1889-1975
Trail Riders (1964/1965)
canvas, 1.426 × 1.880 m (56⅛ × 74 in.)
National Gallery of Art, Washington
Gift of the Artist 1975.42.1

Pierre Bonnard, 1867-1947
Children Leaving School (c. 1895)
cardboard on wood, 0.289 × 0.440 m
(11⅜ × 17⅜ in.)
National Gallery of Art, Washington
Ailsa Mellon Bruce Collection 1970.17.5

Rendered by E. Boyd, c. 1936
Painted Chest (c. 1810-1820)
watercolor, graphite, and gouache
0.281 × 0.368 m (11¹⁄₁₆ × 14½ in.)
Index of American Design 1943.8.7515

Rendered by E. Boyd, c. 1936
Painted Chest (c. 1820)
watercolor, gouache, and graphite
0.247 × 0.357 m (9¾ × 14¹⁄₁₆ in.)
Index of American Design 1943.8.8141

Gustave Caillebotte, 1848-1894
Skiffs (1877)
oil on canvas, 0.889 × 1.162 m (35 × 45¾ in.)
National Gallery of Art, Washington
Collection of Mr. and Mrs. Paul Mellon 1985.64.6

Rendered by Rose Campbell-Gerke, c. 1937
Spur (c. 1890)
watercolor, graphite, colored pencil, and pen and ink
0.279 × 0.354 m (11 × 13¹⁵⁄₁₆ in.)
Index of American Design 1943.8.1860

George Catlin, 1796-1872
Snow Shoe Dance—Ojibbeway (1861/1869)
cardboard, 0.465 × 0.620 m (18⁵⁄₁₆ × 24½ in.)
National Gallery of Art, Washington
Paul Mellon Collection 1965.16.136

Thomas Chambers, 1808-in or after 1866
The Connecticut Valley (mid-19th century)
canvas, 0.457 × 0.610 m (18 × 24 in.)
National Gallery of Art, Washington
Gift of Edgar William and Bernice Chrysler Garbisch
1956.13.2

L. M. Cooke, active c. 1875
Salute to General Washington in New York Harbor
(fourth quarter 19th century)
canvas, 0.686 × 1.022 m (27 × 40¼ in.)
National Gallery of Art, Washington
Gift of Edgar William and Bernice Chrysler Garbisch
1953.5.7

Jean-Baptiste-Camille Corot, 1796-1875
Forest of Fontainebleau (c. 1830)
oil on canvas, 1.756 × 2.426 m (69⅛ × 95½ in.)
National Gallery of Art, Washington
Chester Dale Collection 1963.10.109

Jasper Francis Cropsey, 1823-1900
Autumn—On the Hudson River (1860)
canvas, 1.525 × 2.743 m (60 × 108 in.)
National Gallery of Art, Washington
Gift of the Avalon Foundation 1963.9.1

Edgar Degas, 1834-1917
Woman Ironing (1882)
oil on canvas, 0.813 × 0.660 m (32 × 26 in.)
National Gallery of Art, Washington
Collection of Mr. and Mrs. Paul Mellon 1972.74.1

André Derain, 1880-1954
Charing Cross Bridge, London (1906)
canvas, 0.803 × 1.003 m (31⅝ × 39½ in.)
National Gallery of Art, Washington
John Hay Whitney Collection 1982.76.3

Thomas Eakins, 1844-1916
Baby at Play (1876)
canvas, 0.819 × 1.228 m (32¼ × 48⅜ in.)
John Hay Whitney Collection 1982.76.5

Thomas Eakins, 1844-1916
Study for "Negro Boy Dancing": The Banjo Player
(c. 1878)
oil on canvas mounted on cardboard, 0.508 × 0.387 m
(20 × 15¼ in.)
National Gallery of Art, Washington
Collection of Mr. and Mrs. Paul Mellon 1985.64.16
National Gallery of Art, Washington

Jean-Honoré Fragonard, 1732-1806
The Swing (probably c. 1765)
oil on canvas, 2.159 × 1.855 m (85 × 73 in.)
National Gallery of Art, Washington
Samuel H. Kress Collection 1961.9.17
National Gallery of Art, Washington

Paul Gauguin, 1848-1903
Breton Girls Dancing, Pont-Aven (1888)
oil on canvas, 0.730 × 0.927 m (28¾ × 36½ in.)
National Gallery of Art, Washington
Collection of Mr. and Mrs. Paul Mellon 1983.1.19
National Gallery of Art, Washington

Théodore Géricault, 1791-1824
The Flemish Farrier (1821)
lithograph, 0.226 × 0.314 m (8⅞ × 12⅜ in.)
National Gallery of Art, Washington
Rosenwald Collection 1943.3.4616
National Gallery of Art, Washington

Rendered by Perkins Harnly, 1946
"California Mission Style" Interior (1910-1911)
watercolor, graphite, pen and ink, and gouache
0.565 × 0.778 m (22¼ × 30⅝ in.)
Index of American Design 1943.8.8140
National Gallery of Art, Washington

Childe Hassam, 1859-1935
Allies Day, May 1917 (1917)
canvas, 0.935 × 0.770 m (36¾ × 30¼ in.)
National Gallery of Art, Washington
Gift of Ethelyn McKinney in memory of her brother,
Glen Ford McKinney 1943.9.1
National Gallery of Art, Washington

Edward Hicks, 1780-1849
The Cornell Farm (1848)
canvas, 0.933 × 1.244 m (36¾ × 49 in.)
National Gallery of Art, Washington
Gift of Edgar William and Bernice Chrysler Garbisch
1964.23.4
National Gallery of Art, Washington

Winslow Homer, 1836-1910
Breezing Up (A Fair Wind) (1876)
canvas, 0.615 × 0.970 m (24⅛ × 38⅛ in.)
National Gallery of Art, Washington
Gift of the W. L. and May T. Mellon Foundation
1943.13.1
National Gallery of Art, Washington

Winslow Homer, 1836-1910
Casting, Number Two (1894)
watercolor over graphite, 0.384 × 0.544 m
(15¹⁄₁₆ × 21⁷⁄₁₆ in.)
National Gallery of Art, Washington
Gift of Ruth K. Henschel in memory of her husband,
Charles R. Henschel 1975.92.2
National Gallery of Art, Washington

Winslow Homer, 1836-1910
Under a Palm Tree (1886)
watercolor, 0.383 × 0.309 m (15¹⁄₁₆ × 12⅛ in.)
National Gallery of Art, Washington
Gift of Ruth K. Henschel in memory of her husband,
Charles R. Henschel 1975.92.16
National Gallery of Art, Washington

After Winslow Homer
Christmas Belles (published 1869)
wood engraving, 0.230 × 0.349 m (9¹⁄₁₆ × 13¾ in.)
National Gallery of Art, Washington
Rosenwald Collection 1958.3.23

George Inness, 1825-1894
The Lackawanna Valley (1855)
canvas, 0.860 × 1.275 m (33⅞ × 50¼ in.)
National Gallery of Art, Washington
Gift of Mrs. Huttleston Rogers 1945.4.1

Rendered by Jane Iverson, c. 1936
Wooden Doll (c. 1800)
watercolor, graphite, gouache, and pen and ink
0.354 × 0.278 m (13¹⁵⁄₁₆ × 10¹⁵⁄₁₆ in.)
Index of American Design 1943.8.8144

Rendered by Frank Keane, c. 1939
Banjo Clock (1805-1815)
watercolor, graphite, pen and ink, and colored pencil
0.508 × 0.370 m (20⅟₁₆ × 14⁹⁄₁₆ in.)
Index of American Design 1943.8.4769

Rendered by William Kieckhofel, c. 1939
Spur (c. 1880-1890)
watercolor, graphite, and colored pencil
0.267 × 0.357 m (10½ × 14⅟₁₆ in.)
Index of American Design 1943.8.8139

Gustav Klimt, 1862-1918
Baby (Cradle) (1917/1918)
canvas, 1.109 × 1.104 m (43⅝ × 43½ in.)
National Gallery of Art, Washington
Gift of Otto and Franziska Kallir with the help of the
Carol and Edwin Gaines Fullinwider Fund 1978.41.1

John Marin, 1870-1953
Untitled: Circus (c. 1953)
oil on canvas, 0.559 × 0.711 m (22 × 28 in.)
National Gallery of Art, Washington
Gift of John Marin, Jr. 1986.54.12

Henri Matisse, 1869-1954
Pianist and Checker Players (1924)
oil on canvas, 0.737 × 0.924 m (29 × 36⅜ in.)
National Gallery of Art, Washington
Collection of Mr. and Mrs. Paul Mellon 1985.64.25

Henri Matisse, 1869-1954
The Funeral of Pierrot (published 1947)
color stencil in gouache, 0.421 × 0.648 m
(16½ × 25½ in.)
National Gallery of Art, Washington
Gift of Mr. and Mrs. Andrew S. Keck 1980.8.10

Henri Matisse, 1869-1954
Still Life with Sleeping Woman (1940)
oil on canvas, 0.825 × 1.007 m (32½ × 39⅝ in.)
National Gallery of Art, Washington
Collection of Mr. and Mrs. Paul Mellon 1985.64.26

Rendered by Katharine Merrill, c. 1938
Dancing Girl from Spark's Circus Wagon (c. 1900)
watercolor and graphite
0.504 × 0.294 m (19⅞ × 11⁹⁄₁₆ in.)
Index of American Design 1943.8.8134

Claude Monet, 1840-1926
Bazille and Camille (1865)
canvas, 0.930 × 0.689 m (36⅝ × 27⅛ in.)
National Gallery of Art, Washington
Ailsa Mellon Bruce Collection 1970.17.41

Claude Monet, 1840-1926
The Cradle—Camille with the Artist's Son Jean (1867)
oil on canvas, 1.168 × 0.889 m (46 × 35 in.)
National Gallery of Art, Washington
Collection of Mr. and Mrs. Paul Mellon 1983.1.25

Claude Monet, 1840-1926
Woman with a Parasol—Madame Monet and Her Son
(1875)
oil on canvas, 1.000 × 0.810 m (39⅜ × 31⅞ in.)
National Gallery of Art, Washington
Collection of Mr. and Mrs. Paul Mellon 1983.1.29

Rendered by Raymond E. Noble, c. 1940
Spur (c. 1850)
watercolor, graphite, colored pencil, and pen and ink
0.267 × 0.356 m (10½ × 14 in.)
Index of American Design 1943.8.8137

Frances Flora Bond Palmer, c. 1812-1876
American Winter Scenes: Morning (published 1854)
hand-colored lithograph on wove paper,
0.540 × 0.710 m (21¼ × 28 in.)
National Gallery of Art, Washington
Collection of Mr. and Mrs. Paul Mellon 1985.64.158

Maurice Brazil Prendergast, 1858-1924
Salem Cove (1916)
oil on canvas, 0.613 × 0.765 m (24⅛ × 30⅛ in.)
National Gallery of Art, Washington
Collection of Mr. and Mrs. Paul Mellon 1985.64.33

William Matthew Prior, 1806-1873
Little Miss Fairfield (1850)
canvas, 0.609 × 0.505 m (24 × 19⅞ in.)
National Gallery of Art, Washington
Gift of Edgar William and Bernice Chrysler Garbisch
1971.83.9

John Quidor, 1801-1881
The Return of Rip Van Winkle (c. 1849)
canvas, 1.010 × 1.265 m (39¾ × 49¾ in.)
National Gallery of Art, Washington
Andrew W. Mellon Collection 1942.8.10

Auguste Renoir, 1841-1919
Picking Flowers (1875)
oil on canvas, 0.543 × 0.652 m (21⅜ × 25⅝ in.)
National Gallery of Art, Washington
Ailsa Mellon Bruce Collection 1970.17.61

Rendered by Josephine Romano and Edith Towner,
1936
Doll, "Mollie Bentley" (c. 1886)
watercolor, graphite, and pen and ink
0.359 × 0.267 m (14⅟₁₆ × 10½ in.)
Index of American Design 1943.8.8135

Henry Merwin Shrady, 1871-1922
The Empty Saddle (1900)
bronze, 0.279 × 0.326 × 0.165 m
(11 × 12⅞ × 6½ in.)
National Gallery of Art, Washington
Gift of Joseph Ternbach 1971.1.1

Rendered by Alfred H. Smith, c. 1940
Eagle (19th century)
watercolor, graphite, and colored pencil
0.381 × 0.536 m (15 × 21¹⁄₁₆ in.)
Index of American Design 1943.8.8143

Frank Stella, born 1936
Star of Persia I (1967)
7-color lithograph (aluminum) on English Vellum
Graph paper
Gift of the Woodward Foundation, Washington, D.C.
1976.56.174

Gerard Terborch II, 1617-1681
The Suitor's Visit (c. 1658)
oil on canvas, 0.800 × 0.753 m (31½ × 29⅝ in.)
National Gallery of Art, Washington
Andrew W. Mellon Collection 1937.1.58

Henri de Toulouse-Lautrec, 1864-1901
The Artist's Dog Flèche (c. 1881)
wood, 0.234 × 0.141 m (9¼ × 5½ in.)
National Gallery of Art, Washington
Ailsa Mellon Bruce Collection 1970.17.84

Various Artists
Tailpiece from *Estampes pour servir a l'Histoire des Moeurs
et du Costume* (published 1783)
engraving, 0.533 × 0.364 m (20¹⁵⁄₁₆ × 14¼ in.)
National Gallery of Art, Washington
Widener Collection 1942.9.1789

Rendered by Vera Van Voris, c. 1937
Spur (1840-1850)
watercolor, graphite, colored pencil, pen and ink and
heightening
0.279 × 0.355 m (11 × 14 in.)
Index of American Design 1943.8.1861

Rendered by Wayne White, 1939-1940
Civil War Drum (c. 1860)
watercolor, graphite, colored pencil, and pen and ink
0.539 × 0.390 m (21¼ × 15⅝ in.)
Index of American Design 1943.8.8142

After William John Wilgus
Ichabod Crane and the Headless Horseman (c. 1855)
canvas, 0.533 × 0.767 m (21 × 30¼ in.)
National Gallery of Art, Washington
Gift of Edgar William and Bernice Chrysler Garbisch
1971.83.21

SONG INDEX